D0764427

*Q7.ROW-979*

# BALD EAGLE

Lynn M. Stone

WITHDRAWN

CONTRA COSTA COUNTY LIBRARY

Rourke

3 1901 03704 4627

Publishing LLC
Vero Beach, Florida 32964

© 2004 Rourke Publishing LLC

All rights reserved. No part of this book may be reproduced or utilized in any form or by any means, electronic or mechanical including photocopying, recording, or by any information storage and retrieval system without permission in writing from the publisher.

www.rourkepublishing.com

PHOTO CREDITS:
Cover photo, title page, pp. 4, 6, 7, 12, 14, 16, 18, 19, 20, 22 © Lynn M. Stone; p. 8 courtesy of Library of Congress; p. 13 courtesy of Western History Collections, University of Oklahoma Libraries

Title page: *As if checking out the metal artwork, a bald eagle flies past an eagle-topped weathervane.*

Editor: Frank Sloan

Cover design by Nicola Stratford
Interior design by Heather Scarborough

**Library of Congress Cataloging-in-Publication Data**

ISBN 1-58952-699-6

Printed in the USA

CG/CG

# TABLE OF CONTENTS


The National Bird ....................................5

An American Eagle ..................................10

The Bald Eagle Today..............................18

Glossary ....................................................23

Index..........................................................24

Further Reading ........................................24

Websites to Visit ......................................24

# The National Bird

Probably no bird in America is better known or more loved than the bald eagle. It is, after all, America's national bird and a **symbol** of the United States.

Whether **soaring** or sweeping down for a fish, the bald eagle always commands attention. It has a dark brown body, a white head, and a white tail. It has sharp, deadly **talons** and a knife-sharp, curved beak.

*The bald eagle and the United States flag are both symbols of the nation.*

The bald eagle hasn't started wars or led explorers to new places. But in the 1970s it did help change America's **environmental** history.

*The bald eagle became rare in the 1960s and helped cause changes in the nation's environmental laws.*

*Eagles appear on many U.S. coins and bills.*

The bald eagle has often been shown on American bills and coins. Coins include silver dollars, quarters, half dollars, and others. Many old coins showing the eagle were called "eagles."

In 1782 the handsome bird was placed on the Great **Seal** of the United States. In the years that followed, the bald eagle appeared on several state seals. It appeared on the president's flag and on official **military** patches and papers.

*This painting appeared in Philadelphia in June, 1776, with the words, "In the form of the Goddess of Youth; giving support to the bald eagle."*

# An American Eagle

*The bald eagle appears on the Great Seal of the United States.*

Charles Thomson was probably the person most responsible for bringing the bald eagle to fame. In June, 1782, secretary of Congress Thomson was working on a design for the Great Seal. An earlier design had shown the seal with a crested eagle. Thomson had no problem with an eagle on the seal. But he wanted an *American* eagle.

Americans in 1782, of course, couldn't have known just how American the bald eagle was. America at that time was made up only of 13 Eastern states. In fact, the bald eagle nested in every one of what became the 50 states except Hawaii.

The bald eagle isn't the only North American eagle. The golden eagle lives commonly in North America, too. Young bald eagles, without their white heads and tails, look much like golden eagles.

*The golden eagle likes mountains. It is not a fish-eating bird like the bald eagle.*

*A Cheyenne chief wears a war bonnet of eagle feathers. Today only Native Americans can legally keep eagle feathers.*

But golden eagles also live well beyond North America. The bald eagle rarely leaves North American air space.

Not everyone was delighted with Thomson's choice of bird. Benjamin Franklin was famously against it. He said the bald eagle was "a bird of bad moral character" and "too lazy to fish for himself."

Birds, of course, are not of moral character, good or bad. Franklin was referring to the bald eagle's habit of sometimes eating **carrion**. And it bothered Franklin that bald eagles, like any of the birds of prey, could be chased by songbirds.

*Benjamin Franklin complained that the bald eagle sometimes ate food it didn't catch. Here an eagle feeds on old salmon.*

But Franklin knew more about matters of the nation than he did about birds. The bald eagle was accepted. It was a wise decision. Not only was the bald eagle a handsome and powerful bird, it was also a bird that lived throughout America and much of Canada.

*The handsome bald eagle, a strong, swift bird of prey, was a wise choice for America's national bird.*

# The Bald Eagle Today

In the 1960s and 1970s the bald eagle became increasingly rare in the lower 48 states. Scientists found the problem. It was DDT, a chemical used to control insects. The problem is that DDT can kill animals other than insects.

*DDT caused the bald eagle to disappear from many states.*

*Shooting bald eagles is against the law, but lawbreakers sometimes target them anyway.*

DDT washed from fields into rivers and seas. It poisoned the **prey** of fish, then the fish. Birds like bald eagles that ate fish were also poisoned. Many birds were in trouble. But people feared especially for the bald eagle. They wondered if the country's national bird would become **extinct**.

Thanks largely to the bald eagle's popularity, the wide use of DDT was stopped in the United States. That decision saved the bald eagle. It also saved many other fish-eating birds.

Today the bald eagle again nests in almost every state. The national bird is flying high.

*People's concern for the bald eagle helped bring an end to the use of DDT.*

# Glossary

**carrion** (CAR ee en) — old, rotting flesh

**environmental** (EN vy ren ment el) — having to do with one's surroundings, such as air and water

**extinct** (EKS tinckt) — gone forever

**military** (MIL eh ter ee) — having to do with, or being part of, the nation's armed forces

**prey** (PRAY) — an animal hunted by another animal for food

**seal** (SEEL) — an official emblem or logo, usually of a government

**soaring** (SOR ing) — a high, lazy flight with few wing beats

**symbol** (SIM bel) — a thing that stands for something, such as a flag standing for a country

**talons** (TAL enz) — the clawed toes of birds of prey, such as hawks, eagles, and owls

*Bald eagles return year after year to the same nest and keep adding sticks. Some nests weigh more than 2,000 pounds (907 kilograms)!*

# Index

beak 5
coins 7
DDT 18, 21
eagle, golden 12, 13
fish 19
Franklin, Benjamin 15, 17
Great Seal of the
United States 9, 10
seals 9
talons 5
Thomson, Charles 10

## Further Reading

Find out more about bald eagles with these helpful books:

- Binns, Tristan Boyd. *The Bald Eagle*. Heinemann Library, 2001.
- Hodge, Deborah. *Eagles*. Kids Can Press, 2000.
- Patent, Dorothy Hinshaw. *The Bald Eagle Returns*. Clarion, 2001.
- Wilson, Jon. *American Eagle: The Symbol of America*. Child's World, 1998.

## Websites to Visit

- www.baldeagleinfo.com/eagle/eagle9.html
- endangered.fws.gov/i/b0h.html

## About the Author

Lynn Stone is a talented natural history photographer and writer. Lynn, a former teacher, travels worldwide to photograph wildlife in their natural habitat. He has more than 500 children's books to his credit.